IMAGES
of America

NAPA COUNTY
POLICE

ON THE COVER AND ABOVE: Visible in this 1943 group photograph of the Napa Police Department (NPD) are members of the Navy Shore Patrol. During World War II, the servicemen on shore leave from nearby naval bases at Mare Island and Port Chicago came to Napa. The Shore Patrol worked jointly with the NPD to police them. Napa police chief Eugene Riordan is pictured at the center of the group, in the suit. (Courtesy of the Napa Police Historical Society.)

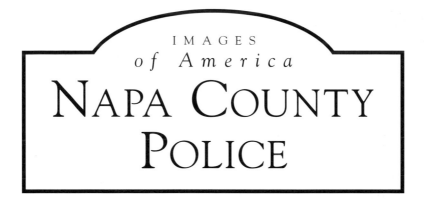

IMAGES
of America

NAPA COUNTY
POLICE

Todd L. Shulman and
the Napa Police Historical Society

ARCADIA
PUBLISHING

Published by Arcadia Publishing
Charleston SC, Chicago IL, Portsmouth NH, San Francisco CA

Printed in the United States of America

Library of Congress Catalog Card Number: 2007920164

For all general information contact Arcadia Publishing at:
Telephone 843-853-2070
Fax 843-853-0044
E-mail sales@arcadiapublishing.com
For customer service and orders:
Toll-Free 1-888-313-2665

Visit us on the Internet at www.arcadiapublishing.com

*To my wife, Stacey, for her many hours of support and understanding
during the research and writing of this book.*

CONTENTS

ACKNOWLEDGMENTS

The Napa Police Historical Society was formed in early 2006 as a way to preserve the history of the Napa Police Department, to honor its current and former employees, and to educate the public about its history. During the course of compiling photographs and artifacts, it became clear to me that the larger story of all Napa County law enforcement needed to be told.

First, this book would not have been possible without the generosity of the many current employees, retirees, concerned citizens, and family members of those who have passed away. A wide variety of people opened their scrapbooks to provide photographs; they also provided vivid memories to help paint the story of the men and women captured on film.

It would be nearly impossible to thank everyone by name; however, I would like to recognize a few individuals who went above and beyond to make this book possible. Former Napa police chief Ken Jennings retrieved many interesting items stored in his seemingly endless collection in his barn. Gwenn McKenzie shared the vast archive of her late husband Bob McKenzie's photographic negative collection, culled from his many years at the *Napa Valley Register*. John Boessenecker and William Secrest, noted Western history writers, provided advice and information from the depth of their experience and research. Napa sheriff's captain Gene Lyerla, California Highway Patrol (CHP) officer Bob Kays, Calistoga police technician Doug O'Neill, St. Helena police sergeant Matt Talbott, Napa Valley College Police Academy director Greg Miraglia, Napa Valley College police chief Ken Arnold, and Napa State Hospital police sergeant Harley Detwiler and detective Jesus Gallegos provided access to their respective departments' history materials.

In addition, the staff of the Napa County Historical Society, California State Archives, and California State Library were invaluable resources and provided access to their respective collections.

Lastly, I would like to thank the many men and women who have served Napa County over the last 150-plus years. Having heard the stories of their bravery and sacrifices, I am proud to count myself among their number. While it would be impossible to include all the images and stories I have gleaned, I hope this book will provide a snapshot into the lives of the many men and women captured on film over the years.

INTRODUCTION

The Napa Valley was first explored by an expedition from the Spanish mission in Sonoma in 1823. At the time, there were six different tribes of Native Americans, numbering around 1,000 people, living in the area. A cholera epidemic in the 1830s wiped out a large percentage of the native population. The valley was first settled by George C. Yount in 1831 after he received a grant of land from the Mexican government. In 1836, Yount built the first log structure built by an American in the territory of California.

Early law enforcement in Napa County was meted out by the *alcalde*, based in the city of Sonoma. Alcaldes were appointed by the Mexican government; they acted as both judge and mayor for the surrounding areas. Until as late as 1850, the area that is now Napa County was considered part of the larger District of Sonoma. In these early days, there were less than 200 non–Native Americans living in the Napa Valley.

Everything in California changed in June 1846 with the Bear Flag Revolt. The revolt started in the city of Sonoma and quickly spread across the state. Unbeknownst to the revolters, the United States declared war against Mexico a month earlier. The two-week-old California Republic decided that it was prudent to allow itself to be annexed into the United States.

From 1846 to 1849, law enforcement was handled by the military government, which had been put in place when Mexico ceded California to the United States.

Organized civilian law enforcement took over in Napa County in 1850, when the county was officially recognized as one of the original 27 counties in the state. The total documented population of the county was 405 souls. Napa County lacked both a courthouse and jail for its first year of existence. Trials were held in either the city of Sonoma or the city of Benicia (the state capital at the time). Prisoners were held in the adobe jail in Sonoma. From these humble beginnings, a few dedicated men would step forward to plant the seed of justice and order in the fertile soil of the Napa Valley.

One

THE EARLY YEARS

The early years of law enforcement in Napa County were an adventure for those brave souls who pinned on a star and strapped on a gun. Napa County became a charter county when California was admitted to the Union in 1850. The county was full of diversity, with a mix of Native Americans, struggling farmers, and disillusioned gold rush miners.

Officers were expected not only to keep order in their towns; they were also tasked with a myriad of ancillary duties. The town marshal had many duties, including collecting taxes, supervising street repairs, acting as animal control officer, and enforcing town codes such as weed control.

Many petty criminals never saw the inside of the county jail, located in the city of Napa. Each township within the county had an elected justice of the peace who meted out punishments in many misdemeanor crimes. Larger towns such as St. Helena and Calistoga had their own jail. The common drunkard or brawler was thrown in the lockup to cool off. Many others served short jail sentences and were admonished to leave town and not come back. In fact, Napa, the largest city in the county, did not have a formal jail until the first courthouse was built in 1856. Prior to this, small-time criminals were chained to the floor on the second floor of the original wood courthouse. Hardened criminals were held in the jail in the city of Sonoma, more than 14 miles away.

These pioneer lawmen paved the way for all those who would protect and serve Napa County over the succeeding 150-plus years; with the barest of training and equipment, they modeled the most important traits for all cops—a heart to help those who could not help themselves and the courage to stand up to those who would prey on the helpless.

Nathaniel McKimmey was appointed as the first sheriff of Napa County in 1850. McKimmey had served as a ferry operator on the Napa River and as a schoolteacher prior to becoming sheriff. He served as Napa County's top cop until 1853. McKimmey left Napa County shortly after, becoming a surveyor in Iowa, Missouri, Kansas, Arkansas, and Oklahoma later in life. McKimmey died in Chandler, Oklahoma, in 1901. (Courtesy of the California State Library.)

A handwritten order signed by California's second governor, John McDougal, was meant to suspend the execution of Hamilton McCauley in 1851. McCauley was under an order of death for killing a justice of the peace in Napa County. The governor sent an emissary with the order from Benicia to Napa. Citizens prevented the emissary from using the ferry to cross the Napa River and lynched McCauley during the night. (Courtesy of the California State Archives.)

John Schull Stark served as Napa's fifth sheriff, from 1855 to 1861. Stark had already distinguished himself by taking part in the third rescue party sent to help the stranded Donner Party in 1847, reportedly carrying two children and supplies to safety. After Stark's stint as sheriff, he went on to serve in the California State Legislature and as a Napa County judge. (Courtesy of Scott Perry.)

The Napa County Courthouse as it appeared c. 1860 looks northwest from the corner of Third and Brown Streets. The first courthouse, built in 1851, was a wood structure located on the same site. It lacked a jail; criminals were either chained to the second-story floor or housed in the Sonoma County jail. The second courthouse (pictured) was built in 1856 and was plagued by structural problems. (Courtesy of the Lawrence and Houseworth Collection of the Society of California Pioneers.)

A bird's-eye view shows the city of Napa in 1871, a year before the city incorporated and four years before the police force was formed. At the time, it was protected by the county sheriff and constables elected to the city's justice court. In 1871, the city's population was about 1,900. (Author's collection.)

Jerome B. Walden was Napa's first chief of police, appointed by the board of trustees in 1875, at the same time the police department was formed. In 1876, the board decided to reorganize the department, eliminating the full-time chief's position. From 1876 to 1909, whoever was elected town marshal was appointed the dual title of chief of police. Walden went on to become a sheriff's deputy and later a shopkeeper. (Courtesy of Crane Walden.)

Thomas Earl was the city of Napa's third marshal, serving from 1874 to 1877. When the police department was reorganized in 1876, he took on the dual title of chief of police. A successful businessman prior to being elected marshal, in 1856 Earl built the first commercial brick building in the city of Napa, hauling the bricks from Sacramento. He also built the first concrete building in Napa County. (Author's collection.)

THOMAS EARL.

Cornelius Nash served as a constable in Calistoga for two years before the town incorporated in 1886. At that time, Nash became its first town marshal; he held the post for 10 years. Nash came to Napa via wagon train in 1847, in the same train as the ill-fated Donner Party, splitting from them prior to crossing the Sierra Nevada. Marshal Nash built the first school in Calistoga. (Author's collection.)

Henry Baddeley served in several jobs protecting the citizens of Napa County. From 1877 to 1881, he was a Napa police officer. He then was elected as a constable and finally served as the Napa County undersheriff. In between catching criminals, Baddeley had time to father 12 children. This photograph is believed to be the earliest photograph of a Napa police officer in uniform; Baddeley's hat badge reads "patrol police." (Courtesy of Kenneth Wallace.)

With the advent of electricity came the first means of communication for law enforcement. Napa installed several lights at key intersections in the city, not for traffic control but to notify the officers they were needed back at the police station; the light would be illuminated red to warn the officers. This view shows one of the signal lights, at the intersection of Main and First Streets. (Courtesy of the Napa County Historical Society.)

John Hall Allison was elected as the first marshal of St. Helena in 1876. He supervised the building of the town's first jail during the same year; the total cost of the structure was $158. Allison had traveled to California from Missouri first in 1951, returning again with his wife and family in 1866. In addition to being marshal, Allison served as the superintendent of streets. (Courtesy of Robert Allison.)

Timothy N. Mount served as a Napa city constable in the 1880s. Constables were elected within each township of Napa County to serve the justice court of that township. Although their primary duties were serving legal paperwork, they frequently acted in the role of a police officer. Later in life, Mount formed the Napa Building and Loan Company. (Author's collection.)

Napa city constable George David Secord is pictured in this late-1890s portrait. Secord was a well-known and well-liked "beat cop" who patrolled the town either on foot or via a horse and buggy. Secord served as a constable until 1909, when he joined the newly reorganized Napa Police Department. (Courtesy of Michael McNab.)

Napa County's longtime jailer was William "Wall" Kennedy, pictured here in a staged 1899 photograph. Kennedy, whose nickname was "Old Desperate," served as the jailer from 1879 to 1900. He also supervised the "chain gang," which completed many public works projects in the city of Napa. Kennedy was a prolific storyteller; one of his most famous stories detailed how he herded a hive of bees across the plains from Missouri to California, using them as a defense against hostile Native Americans along the way. (Courtesy of the Napa County Historical Society.)

Two

THE NAPA COUNTY SHERIFF'S DEPARTMENT

The Napa County Sheriff's Department was formed in 1850 as one of the first acts of the Napa County Board of Supervisors; Nathaniel McKimmey was elected Napa's first sheriff. The department consisted of two people: Sheriff McKimmey and one undersheriff. They policed a county covering more than 700 square miles; the entire population of the county at the time was estimated to be 450. The first known lynching in Napa County occurred in Sheriff McKimmey's first year on the job.

During the past 157 years, there have been 25 elected sheriffs. The population of the county has grown to over 124,000.

Throughout its history, the sheriff's department has enlisted the aid of allied agencies to help cover the vast county. Early on, this aid came in the form of town marshals and constables. Later city police and the highway patrol pitched in.

Besides patrolling the unincorporated areas of the county, the sheriff's department has also historically performed various other duties, including acting as court bailiffs, serving civil papers, running the mounted posse, and presiding over executions (the last of which occurred in 1897). In modern times, the department has also added other duties, including running the bomb squad, dive team, off-road enforcement team, aero squadron, SWAT team, and search-and-rescue team. The department also ran the county jail until 1975, when the separate department of corrections was formed. In addition, the sheriff's department currently provides contracted police services to two cities within the county, Yountville and American Canyon.

For the first 125 years of its history, the sheriff's department was housed in the historic county courthouse, which still stands at 825 Brown Street, in the city of Napa. In 1976, the department moved into the newly constructed hall of justice located across the street; the building was quickly outgrown. In 2005, the department moved into a new building in the southern part of the county at 1535 Airport Road, which includes a state-of-the-art coroner's facility.

Today the Napa County Sheriff's Department is staffed by 109 sworn and 27 support personnel. The current sheriff is Doug Koford.

This is an example of the early badge worn by Napa County sheriff's deputies. It was a "tin star," a silver-colored, six-point star. Today's deputies wear a standard seven-point gold badge with the California state seal in the center. (Author's collection.)

Charles H. Allen served as sheriff from 1862 to 1864. During his term, he arrested James Gilbert Jenkins for murdering Jenkins's girlfriend's father during an argument; Jenkins was convicted and sentenced to hang for the crime. Sheriff Allen transcribed Jenkins's account of his life of crime while he awaited his date with the hangman. In the transcript, which was later published, Jenkins claimed he had murdered 8 white men and 10 Native Americans. (Courtesy of the Napa County Sheriff's Department.)

The Napa County Courthouse as it appeared c. 1900 looks northwest from the corner of Third and Brown Streets. Built in 1879, this was the third courthouse. The building served not only as a courthouse but also as the headquarters for the Napa County Sheriff's Department and as the county's main jail. In 1976, the county moved the sheriff's department, jail, and some courtrooms to the newly constructed hall of justice across Third Street. A state-of-the-art courthouse was constructed next to the hall of justice in 1999. Despite these additional buildings, the historic courthouse still stands today in downtown Napa, minus the cupola, which was removed in the 1930s. It houses several courtrooms, court offices, and serves as a marshaling area for jurors. (Courtesy of the Napa County Historical Society.)

An unidentified Napa deputy sheriff is pictured at the beginning of the 20th century in the standard uniform of the time: a badge on the left breast. Law enforcement in Napa County would not take on standardized uniforms until the early 1900s. The earliest known Napa Sheriff uniforms date to the 1920s. (Courtesy of Mike Vanwormer.)

John P. Steckter served as sheriff from 1926 to 1944. On August 17, 1929, Steckter and Deputy Howard Westendorf confronted a transient known as the "Mount Veeder Terrorist," a man who had been trespassing at nearby ranches. A shoot-out ensued, with Westendorf saving Steckter's life by shooting and killing the suspect. Steckter retired with two years left on his last term amid a grand jury investigation into misappropriated funds. Board of Supervisors president Joseph Moore took over the last two years of Steckter's term. (Courtesy of the Napa County Sheriff's Department.)

Sheriff John Claussen began his law enforcement career with the Napa Police, serving there from 1938 to 1943. He was appointed undersheriff in 1944 and was elected sheriff in 1946. Claussen was instrumental in expanding services that the sheriff's department provided, including starting the graveyard shift, creating the aero squadron and mounted posse, and initiating a juvenile officer program. (Courtesy of the Robert E. McKenzie collection of the Napa Police Historical Society.)

This photograph from 1952 shows the size of the department led by Sheriff John Claussen (third row, fourth from left). Undersheriff Wes Gardner, in the dark shirt, is at the far left. Gardner was a Napa police officer during the 1930s and 1940s. During the 1950s, deputies worked until 2:00 a.m., then would go home and be on-call. A formal graveyard shift did not start until 1963. (Courtesy of the Napa County Sheriff's Department.)

Sheriff's aero squad members discuss a search pattern in this 1950s photograph. The aero squad was formed in 1949 by Sheriff John Claussen. It consists of volunteer pilots who perform aerial searches, surveillance for criminal activity, and prisoner transports. (Courtesy of the Napa County Sheriff's Department.)

Members of the mounted posse prepare for firing range training in 1952. Training the posse were Deputy Paul Amen (center) and Undersheriff Wesley Gardner (to the right of Amen, holding pistol). Amen and Gardner both served as Napa police officers before becoming sheriff's deputies; they were both known as expert shots and ran the sheriff's marksmanship program. (Courtesy of the Napa County Sheriff's Department.)

Deputy Mike Chouinard inspects the damage to the jail after a breakout late in the 1950s. At the time, Chouinard was the sole person assigned to jail duty and the only deputy on duty in the county. The breakout was discovered when the escapee's mother phoned Chouinard to find out why her son was collecting his clothes from her house. Chouinard had a Napa police officer watch the jail's command center while he discovered how the escape occurred. In the photograph at right, Chouinard points out the iron bars in the ceiling, which were sawed through. In the photograph below, he looks over the hole in the roof that the escapee climbed out of. (Courtesy of Mike Chouinard.)

Air Force sergeant Harold Moak (left) directs sheriff's deputies Joe Page (center) and John Dellagana (right) to the site of a B-25 airplane crash in 1954. The plane crashed in the Monticello area of Napa County; all eight crewmen onboard were killed. Moak was part of the search-and-rescue effort and had parachuted into the area of the crash. (Courtesy of the Napa County Sheriff's Department.)

Det. Hal Snook served as the sheriff department's first evidence technician; he and Napa police sergeant Chuck Hansen pioneered crime scene investigation (CSI) work in Napa County. Snook is shown in this photograph with his signature smoking pipe; he reportedly quit smoking it on the day he retired. Here Snook is using a specialized camera to make a copy of a yearbook photograph. (Courtesy of the Napa County Sheriff's Department.)

Deputy Joe Meyer receives medical aid after a 1957 accident at the intersection of Freeway Drive and First Street in the city of Napa. The vehicle that Deputies Meyer and Don Jones struck is visible in the background, resting on its roof. (Courtesy of the Robert E. McKenzie collection of the Napa Police Historical Society.)

A worker applies the final decals onto the sheriff's first patrol boat. The boat was put into service in 1959 and was used at Lake Berryessa, a recreation area in eastern Napa County. The use of Lake Berryessa has grown steadily as people from throughout the Bay Area come to unwind. The sheriffs at Lake Berryessa currently have a resident deputy, five boat patrols, and two personal watercraft. (Courtesy of the Napa County Sheriff's Department.)

Sheriff Earl Randol entered Napa County law enforcement as an officer at the Napa Police Department in 1952. He served there until he was elected sheriff in 1967. In 1969, the elected position of coroner was merged into the sheriff's duties, making Randol the first sheriff-coroner of Napa County. Randol served as sheriff until 1979. (Courtesy of the Napa County Sheriff's Department.)

In 1967, Capt. Joe Page (foreground) saw the need for officers to have a means to send and receive radio messages while outside their patrol cars, such as during traffic stops; this was in an era before portable walkie-talkie use by police. Page, along with county communications director Allen Wong (background), developed a combination speaker/microphone that mounted to the front fender of a patrol car. (Courtesy of the Napa County Sheriff's Department.)

While this photograph may look disturbing, it is merely the end of a successful 1967 training exercise. Members of the sheriff's mounted posse took part in the mock search for a wanted murderer. The posse uses mounted officers and bloodhounds to search for both missing persons and wanted persons. (Courtesy of the Napa County Sheriff's Department.)

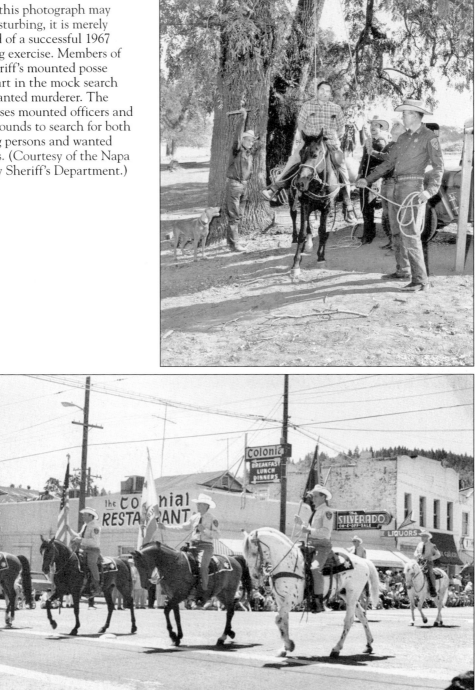

The mounted posse was formed in 1949; it is the oldest continually working posse in California. The posse's primary duty is to assist with rural search-and-rescue operations, although it has also been activated to help during local emergencies, such as during the periodic flooding of the Napa River. They have also acted as ambassadors of the sheriff, as in this 1969 parade in Calistoga. (Courtesy of the Napa County Sheriff's Department.)

Members of the sheriff's basketball team pose before their 1970 benefit game versus the Napa Police Department team. The match was planned in order to raise money for the Napa County Peace Officer Association's widows and orphans fund. The police department won the game. (Courtesy of the Napa County Sheriff's Department.)

Sheriff Earl Randol (left) presents an honorary deputy sheriff identification card to Joe Riggins. In 1973, Riggins was in Napa County filming one of many television commercials in the role of a sheriff. Riggins's most famous tagline was, "You in a heap of trouble, boy." (Courtesy of the Napa County Sheriff's Department.)

The hall of justice opened in 1976. It was meant to replace the former jail, which had been condemned by the fire marshal. The building also housed courtrooms and the sheriff's department. The jail portion was expanded further in 1984. In 1999, a separate courthouse was built on the land at the upper left. The sheriff's department moved to its current building, off of Airport Road, in 2005. (Courtesy of the Napa County Sheriff's Department.)

Constable Lamar "Topsy" Tallman served as the last constable for the city of Napa from 1966 until the mid-1970s, when the position was absorbed into the sheriff's department. Napa County marshals took over duties of acting as bailiffs in the courts until 2001, when they too were absorbed into the sheriff's department. (Courtesy of the Napa County Sheriff's Department.)

A mid-1970s sheriff's patrol car is about to be towed after being involved in a traffic accident. It is fair to assume that the sheriff was not happy; the vehicle was brand-new, as evidenced by the temporary registration in the rear window. This photograph also shows the short-lived black-and-white color scheme used; for most of its history, the sheriff's department has used completely white vehicles. (Courtesy of the Napa County Sheriff's Department.)

Deputy Dave Glover working as dispatcher/jailer. Until the mid-1970s, a sworn deputy manned the radio, took calls, and monitored the inmates within the county jail. Calls for service were recorded on reel-to-reel tapes, and the information was documented using a manual typewriter. (Courtesy of the Napa County Sheriff's Department.)

Three consecutive Napa County sheriffs pose in this 1970s photograph. From left to right are Earl Randol (1967–1979), Joseph Moore (1944–1946), and John Claussen (1946–1967). A picnic was held at Lake Berryessa annually in honor of Sheriff Moore's birthday. (Courtesy of the Napa County Sheriff's Department.)

The Sheriff's SWAT team was formed in 1975 and was the first in Napa County. Members were, from left to right, (first row) Rick Andersen and Dick Hathaway; (second row) Mel Fechter, Gar Harry, and Tom Butler Jr. Andersen was the department's historian and built the museum within the new sheriff's department in 2005. (Courtesy of Rick Andersen.)

In 1977, Deputy Richard Hathaway and Bo became the first K-9 team in Napa County. Within two years, the sheriff's department would have three teams on duty and the Napa Police Department would have one. Today both agencies, along with the St. Helena Police Department, field teams. (Courtesy of Richard Hathaway.)

The department is pictured as it was under the reign of Sheriff Phillip "Bucky" Stewart (first row, eighth from left), who was elected in 1979 and served until 1986. He instituted the department's K-9 program and assigned two deputies as motorcycle officers. Sheriff Stewart, a cattle rancher, also sent several deputies to training courses concerning rural crimes investigations, such as cattle rustling. (Courtesy of the Napa County Sheriff's Department.)

Deputy Mel Atkins poses astride his Kawasaki Police 1000 motorcycle in this mid-1980s photograph. Sheriff Bucky Stewart implemented a short-lived traffic unit within the sheriff's department, which consisted of two motorcycle deputies. The next deputies to write traffic tickets from a motorcycle would not appear until 2003, when the contracted police department in the city of American Canyon began using them. (Courtesy of the Napa County Sheriff's Department.)

Sheriff Gary Simpson served 17 years with the Napa Police Department before being elected sheriff in 1986. During his 20 years as sheriff, he oversaw the computerization of the department, instituted the drug abuse resistance education (DARE) program in county schools, and saw the creation of two contract police departments staffed by sheriff's personnel, in the cities of Yountville and American Canyon. (Courtesy of the Napa County Sheriff's Department.)

The Napa County Sheriff's Department moved to its current location on Airport Road in 2005. The facility includes a state-of-the-art coroner's office, eco-friendly design, and built-in unused space to allow for growth of the department. In addition to this facility, the sheriff's department's contracted police departments have their own facilities: there is a substation in the city of Yountville and a stand-alone public safety building is currently being built in the city of American Canyon. (Author's collection.)

Three

THE NAPA
POLICE DEPARTMENT

The Napa Police Department was formed in 1875, three years after the city of Napa was incorporated. At the time, the city had a population of 2,000. Prior to that time, the city was policed by an elected marshal and constable. The department initially consisted of Chief of Police Jerome B. Walden, two police officers, and two night watchmen. After a year, the board of trustees decided to save the chief's $100-a-month salary by appointing the marshal as the chief of police. There were nine marshals who also served as the chief of police.

In 1909, the city board of trustees abolished the position of marshal and made the last marshal, N. E. Boyd, the first full-time chief of police. At the time, Chief Boyd was in charge of three officers. Documents from the time indicate officers were to be uniformed as follows: a slouch hat with braid around the band, a blue double-breasted coat with a double row of brass buttons, and a star-shaped badge on the left breast area.

After Chief Boyd retired in 1919, the board of trustees engaged in a contentious fight over how to replace him. In a divided vote, the board decided to appoint then–fire chief Charles Otterson to the dual position of chief of police. Chief Otterson held the dual title for three years, housing the police department in the second story of the fire station.

Both the population of Napa and the size of the Napa Police Department exploded during World War II. The growth of nearby Mare Island Naval Station and Port Chicago caused an influx of war industry workers and service personnel on leave. In fact, during the war, police officers patrolled jointly with navy shore patrol officers to combat the routine fights that broke out at the bars on Main Street.

Gradually the department grew and was organized into various bureaus, including traffic enforcement, investigations, and youth services. Today the Napa Police Department employs 75 sworn officers and 67 support personnel. It serves a city of over 75,000 people. The current chief of police is Richard Melton.

Charles Otterson, a firefighter by trade, served as a "special police officer" with the Napa Police starting in 1907. This was akin to a reserve officer, helping when the regular officers needed assistance. In 1919, Otterson, the then–Napa fire chief, was also appointed as the chief of police by the city council. He served in the dual role for three years. (Courtesy of the Napa Firefighter's Museum.)

Officer Lafayette "Lafe" Smith (center) poses in the Hillman Cigar Store in this 1911 photograph. Smith is flanked by building contractor Henry Vienop (left) and cigar maker Otto Koch (right). In 1959, Vienop served as the building contractor during the construction of the current police station on First Street. Officer Smith primarily served as the town's night watchman during his 25-year career. (Courtesy of Alma Skillings.)

Chief Nathanial Ellington Boyd was the last person to hold the dual titles of Napa town marshal and chief of police. He was elected marshal in 1907. In 1909, the city council abolished the marshal's position and kept Chief Boyd as Napa's first full-time police chief. (Courtesy of the Napa Police Historical Society.)

Officer George W. Wooden was one of three officers working for the department in 1913. He served alongside Officers Fred Hein and George Secord, under the direction of Chief N. E. Boyd. Officers of the time were hired for their trustworthiness and their size; many times, they worked solo and had to be able to take care of themselves in a fight. Wooden was a descendant of John Wooden, for whom the Wooden Valley area of Napa County is named. (Courtesy of the Napa Police Historical Society.)

Officer George David Secord (center) "puts the collar" on two friends, Stanley Steele (left) and Fred Levy (right) in this 1913 photograph. Secord wore badge No. 1. There had been other officers before Secord; however, he was the first appointed under the newly reorganized department in 1909. This photograph illustrates the uniform of the time, which included a helmet-style hat and a wool coat. Officers' firearms were concealed under the coats; their primary compliance tool was a large wooden baton carried prominently. (Courtesy of Claire Erks.)

This 1928 shows the department under the helm of Chief Alexander Herritt (center). Officers are wearing silver six-point star badges. In 2000, the department's official badge was changed from a standard seven-point gold badge back to this style in honor of the department's 125th anniversary. (Courtesy of the Napa County Historical Society.)

Alexander Herritt served as chief from 1922 until his untimely death in 1933. Chief Herritt was returning to the police station on Brown Street after answering a call for service when he suffered a massive heart attack. Chief Herritt was able to turn the ignition off and safely maneuver the patrol car to the curb. He is one of two officers to die in the line of duty. (Courtesy of the Napa Police Historical Society.)

One of Napa Police Department's first traffic enforcement officers, Ed Glos, is pictured on his 1933 Harley-Davidson. Officer Glos's revolver, now on display at the police station, was hand-engraved by an inmate at the county jail. The Napa Police Traffic Division currently is staffed with four officers and a sergeant. Their current duty motorcycles are made by BMW. (Courtesy of the Napa Police Historical Society.)

This photograph of Capt. Constance "Dell" Dellamadalena illustrates several distinctive 1930s uniform elements: the shield-type badge used briefly by the NPD, the Sam Browne belt with shoulder strap, and a dark blue wool uniform. Dellamadalena served as the department's second captain during the 1940s. His son, Frank, became an officer in 1952. (Courtesy of the Napa Police Historical Society.)

Sherwood Munk posed for this photograph shortly after being hired, in 1936. A native of Napa, Munk worked his way up the ranks from patrolman to chief during his 31-year career at the department. Three of his sons went on to serve in law enforcement as well. (Courtesy of the Napa Police Historical Society.)

The Napa Police station during the 1930s until 1952 was located on Brown Street, between Second and Third Streets, across the street from the historic courthouse. Chief of Police Eugene Riordan is visible in this 1939 photograph. The department's fleet of vehicles (a Ford Tudor and a Harley-Davidson) is also visible. Later the garage portion of the station was converted to afford more office space. (Courtesy of the Napa Police Historical Society.)

The interior of the police station is seen as it appeared in 1939. An officer was assigned to work at the station; he took information from citizens who walked in or called via phone. At the time, there was only one-way communications with patrol cars. If an officer had a question about a radio call, he would have to pull over and find a pay phone. (Courtesy of the Napa Police Historical Society.)

Officer John Claussen patrols the streets of Napa in the early 1940s. Claussen worked at the department for five years before being appointed Napa County undersheriff in 1943. He was elected sheriff in 1946 and served as Napa County's top cop until 1966, when he lost his fifth election bid to Earl Randol, another former police officer. (Courtesy of the Napa County Sheriff's Department.)

A large portion of the entire department is visible in this 1949 photograph taken at the police station on Brown Street. The officers are, from left to right, Howard Westendorf, Jack Blair, Elmer Stahl, Owen Roberts, and Art Corbett. Westendorf and Roberts were retirees hired back as extra help during World War II; they both stayed on until the early 1950s. (Courtesy of the Napa Police Historical Society.)

Three future leaders of the NPD are, from left to right, Art Corbett, Sherwood Munk, and Jack Blair. In this 1949 photograph, they are pictured in front of the police station on Brown Street. Corbett became a captain and was responsible for redesigning the department's shoulder patch in 1952. Munk became chief in 1952, serving until 1967; Blair served as Munk's assistant chief. (Courtesy of the Napa Police Historical Society.)

The traffic unit poses for this 1949 photograph at Fuller Park in downtown Napa. The officers are, from left to right, Andy Blythe, Jack Johnson, Emil Imboden, and Willis Hill. Officer Blythe rode the three-wheel Harley-Davidson servi-car motorcycle and was the department's first parking enforcement officer. (Courtesy of the Napa Police Historical Society.)

Emil "Ham" Imboden (left) and Dewey Burnsed wear the two common styles of uniforms used during the 1940s and 1950s. Imboden sports the "Ike" jacket, named after a style made popular by Dwight D. Eisenhower during World War II. Burnsed is wearing a stylish black leather jacket; it featured integrated buckles along the bottom edge that could be used to hold the officer's duty belt. (Courtesy of the Napa Police Historical Society.)

Officer Jack Crowley investigates a fatal traffic accident on Fifth Street, near Main Street, in this 1955 photograph. At the time, the "Hatt building" was still an active grain mill; the building was redeveloped in 2000 into a boutique hotel and restaurants. Today major accidents such as this one are investigated by a team of officers known as the traffic accident reconstruction team. (Courtesy of the Napa Police Historical Society.)

High school student Don Self (left) is shown a patrol car by Chief Sherwood Munk during 1956 "youth day"; one day a year, high school students would work in various departments within the city. Although the patrol car lacked many identifying features common in today's vehicles, the large public-address speaker on the roof would have been hard to miss. (Courtesy of the Robert E. McKenzie collection of the Napa Police Historical Society.)

Members of the Napa Police Department pose with their vehicles in 1957. At the time, the police department was located on Fifth Street, just east of Brown Street. The department moved to its current building in 1959. The former police station now houses a day spa. The present-day Napa City-County Library is located at the site of the warehouse visible at the right of this photograph. (Courtesy of the Robert E. McKenzie collection of the Napa Police Historical Society.)

Officer Glenn Kingsford (left) and Ken Jennings prepare for patrol in 1957. Officer Kingsford wears a tan uniform, denoting that he was one of the department's reserve officers. He went on to become a full-time officer and was later the last person to hold the full-time detective position. After Detective Kingsford retired, his position was converted to a four-year, rotating assignment. (Courtesy of the Napa Police Historical Society.)

Members of the department posed for this 1957 photograph in front of the police station on Fifth Street. The size of the force has more than tripled in the last 50 years; the number of support personnel has grown to more than 60 people. (Courtesy of the Napa Police Historical Society.)

Assistant chief Jack Blair investigates a burglary in 1958. News reports from the 1940s and 1950s revealed a high number of safecracking crimes carried out by "yeggs" (slang for a safecracker). Prior to the 1960s, the department did not employ detectives; the chief or assistant chief stepped in to investigate major crimes. (Courtesy of the Robert E. McKenzie collection of the Napa Police Historical Society.)

Napa's first policewomen were Derelys "Chickie" McCuen (left) and Gladys "Pat" Botts (right). The "Meter Mollies," as they were known, were first hired in 1958 and had many hats; they acted as police matrons when dealing with female prisoners and filled in as police clerk-dispatchers, as well as doing their main job, writing parking tickets. The first full-time female police officer at the NPD was appointed in 1977. (Courtesy of the Robert E. McKenzie collection of the Napa Police Historical Society.)

The current Napa Police station, located on First Street just west of School Street, is pictured as it looked when it was dedicated in 1959. A second story was added to the building in 1974. The building was further enlarged in 1992. The department is currently considering either further remodeling or relocating to a new facility because of a lack of space. (Courtesy of the Robert E. McKenzie collection of the Napa Police Historical Society.)

In 1959, this room served several purposes in the newly built police station. It was the locker room for the then-male-only patrol force, the briefing room for patrol shifts hitting the streets, and the report writing room. (Courtesy of the Robert E. McKenzie collection of the Napa Police Historical Society.)

The police reserve program began in 1956. Officers wore khaki uniforms and were issued seven-point silver badges. They were required to volunteer at least eight hours per month and be available in case of emergencies. Several reserve officers went on to become full-time officers. The program was disbanded in the 1980s when the state changed the training requirements. (Courtesy of the Robert E. McKenzie collection of the Napa Police Historical Society.)

Officer Chuck Hansen poses with members of the Napa Junior Traffic Patrol in 1958. The program, which is still active, began in 1955. It uses volunteers from the various elementary schools in Napa to act as crossing guards. At the end of the school year, participants gather for a review at Napa Memorial Stadium. The father of Dominic Elia (standing, far left) was an officer with the Napa Police, and his daughter is currently serving as an officer. (Courtesy of the Napa Police Historical Society.)

Sgt. Dewey Burnsed acts as dispatcher and call taker in this 1959 photograph. Prior to 1961, the Napa police employed police clerk-dispatchers; however, officers performed these duties after normal business hours. Also visible is a "Conalert" emergency radio, a civil-defense system in place in the 1950s during the cold war; it was the precursor to the emergency broadcast system. (Courtesy of the Robert E. McKenzie collection of the Napa Police Historical Society.)

Officer Emil "Ham" Imboden admires the newly completed shooting range in 1961. The area, a former quarry for the Basalt Rock Company, is still used today by the department, although it has been remodeled several times. The current range uses a backstop area filled with recycled tire chips to stop and mitigate contamination from the fired bullets. (Courtesy of the Robert E. McKenzie collection of the Napa Police Historical Society.)

Carolynn Jolliffe assists an officer with the child of a crime victim. Although Jolliffe and the other Meter Mollies' primary duty was enforcing parking laws, they were frequently called on to act as police matrons, helping deal with female offenders and juvenile crime victims. Parking enforcement duties were later transferred from the police to the city's finance department. (Courtesy of the Napa Police Historical Society.)

In 1965, the Napa County Independent Insurance Agents Association donated a working scale model of a traffic signal to the department for use in a traffic safety campaign. Officer Chuck Holden used the device in his role supervising the junior traffic patrol. (Courtesy of the Robert E. McKenzie collection of the Napa Police Historical Society.)

A Dodge Polara leads a mid-1960s parade on Third Street in downtown Napa. At the time, patrol cars used a single red "bubble gum" light on the roof; red-and-blue light bars would not be introduced until the early 1970s. Visible in the background is the Uptown Theater, a classic movie theater that went out of business with the advent of the multiplex; it is currently under renovation. (Courtesy of the Napa Police Historical Society.)

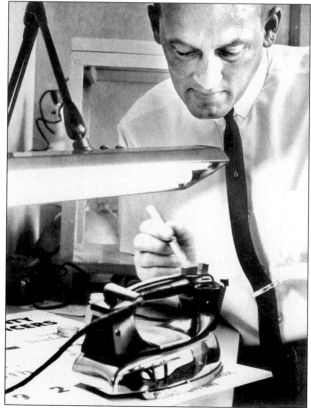

Sgt. Chuck Hansen fingerprints evidence in a murder investigation in 1965. Sergeant Hansen was a pioneer of in-house fingerprint analysis and evidence collection in Napa County. After 29 years of service, he retired in 1983. Today the Napa Police and Sheriff's Departments both have full-time civilian forensic specialists. The NPD also employs crime scene specialists, officers who are cross-trained in evidence collection. (Courtesy of the Napa Police Historical Society.)

Det. Ron Montgomery (left) and police clerk Carolynn Jolliffe work together to document a crime scene in 1967. Montgomery was one of two full-time detectives, along with Glenn Kingsford. He is using a Graflex camera, which produced 4-by-5-inch black-and-white negatives. Currently the department utilizes digital camera technology. (Courtesy of the Napa Police Historical Society.)

The entire department posed for this photograph shortly after Ken Jennings (center, in uniform and wearing a tie) took over as chief in 1968. Jennings joined the force in 1955 and rose to the rank of sergeant before being appointed chief. He led the department until his retirement in 1987. (Courtesy of the Napa Police Historical Society.)

Prior to formalized field training programs, new officers received hands-on instruction from senior officers. In this 1970 photograph, Officer Bob Vanwormer (second from left) instructs new officers on the use of a radar "speedalyzer" unit. The new officers are, from left to right, Gary Simpson, Dan Lonergan, and Paul Cline. Gary Simpson would go on to serve as Napa County sheriff from 1986 to 2006. (Courtesy of the Napa Police Historical Society.)

New employee Cora Steeves (left) receives training in fingerprinting techniques from police clerk Carolynn Jolliffe in this 1970 photograph. Steeves is currently entering her 37th year at the department, working in the records bureau. (Courtesy of the Napa Police Historical Society.)

The Napa Police Department was decorated in 1971, not by an antiestablishment group but by a group of Napa High School students to show support for law enforcement. The banner on the front of the building reads, "If you don't like COPS the next time you need help call a hippie!" (Courtesy of the Napa Police Historical Society.)

Sgt. George Donald poses in the newly adopted all-navy-blue uniform in this 1974 photograph. Prior to this time, officers wore a light-gray shirt and navy-blue pants. Donald would later rise to the rank of deputy chief before retiring in 1996. Visible in the background is a Dodge Monaco police car; it sports a short-lived all-white color scheme. (Courtesy of Ria Donald.)

This 1976 photograph shows the equipment available to the patrol officer of the time. Today's vehicles have become mobile computer platforms filled with modern technologies such as dashboard video cameras, mobile data computers, cellular telephones, and global positioning systems. (Courtesy of the Napa Police Historical Society.)

This makeshift film studio was used by the department in the 1970s to document field sobriety tests given to suspected drunk drivers. At the right is a first-generation breath-testing machine. This "studio" was located in the basement of the department. Suspected drunk drivers performed for the camera here on the way to the county jail. (Courtesy of the Napa Police Historical Society.)

The community relations van was converted from a delivery truck into a mobile public relations tool by Sgt. Joe Masel and Sgt. Bill Niles in 1972. The van featured displays of drug paraphernalia, confiscated weapons, and Napa police history items. In this 1976 photograph, the van is decked out in celebration of the bicentennial. (Courtesy of the Napa Police Historical Society.)

The records bureau is pictured in 1976; visible at the right is the strip-file master name index. Prior to the advent of computers, every person contacted by officers was noted in this index. In 2006, the department switched to a paperless report writing system. Data on persons contacted can now be accessed by officers via mobile data computers in their patrol cars. (Courtesy of the Napa Police Historical Society.)

Police dispatcher Karen Blakesly is on the job in 1976. Visible are the manual punch cards, which dispatchers used to log the activities of patrol officers. A card was punched in an electronic time clock when an event of interest was logged. (Courtesy of the Napa Police Historical Society.)

The department's first K-9, Vem, entered service in 1978. Tragically, in 1979, Vem was stabbed and killed by a suspect while protecting his handler, John O'Donnell. The incident spurred a police sick-out, or "blue flu," and made national headlines when the judge let the suspect out of jail on a low bail amount. O'Donnell received letters of support from people all over the country. (Courtesy of John O'Donnell.)

The department's first SWAT team was formed in 1978. Pictured here are the original members—from left to right, Ruben Faria, Bruce Baker, Vince Deguilio, Randy Bowman, and Gary Simpson. The current SWAT team consists of a sergeant and 11 members, including a combat medic. Attached to the team are also six hostage negotiators. The team works closely with the Napa County Sheriff's SWAT team. (Courtesy of the Napa Police Historical Society.)

In 1986, the department acquired this Bell Model 47 helicopter as surplus equipment from the federal government. Deputy chief Gary Domingo organized the acquisition, and Napa firefighter Bob Nance acted as pilot. The program was short-lived because of maintenance costs. Currently the CHP provides helicopter and fixed-wing aircraft support to Napa County. (Courtesy of the Napa Police Historical Society.)

This 1991 Chevy Camaro served briefly as one of the department's traffic enforcement units. The vehicle shows the standard markings of patrol cars from the late 1980s until 1995; it featured the city's burgundy logo and black block lettering. (Courtesy of the Napa Police Historical Society.)

K-9s Max (left) and Wolf prepare to pull Santa's patrol car in this 2000 photograph. This image was sent as a Christmas card to officers and friends by the K-9 officers at the time, Amy Held (Hunter) and Debbie Peecook. (Courtesy of the Napa Police Historical Society.)

Community service officer Chris Baker (Nunley) demonstrates the proper installation of a car seat to a meeting of Hispanic parents. Baker has inspected thousands of car seats over the last 10 years during various community meetings and drive-in inspection events throughout Napa County and beyond. (Courtesy of Chris Nunley).

Chief Dan Monez led the department from 1986 to 2004. He served as a lieutenant in the Solano County Sheriff's Department before being appointed. Chief Monez oversaw the computerization of the department and implemented a community-oriented policing program. (Courtesy of the Napa Police Historical Society.)

Richard Melton has been the chief of police since 2004. He formerly served as the chief in the New Mexico cities of Farmington and Los Alamos. Chief Melton has overseen the department's transition to a paperless report writing system and is working on several high-tech programs to enhance the department's effectiveness. (Courtesy of the Napa Police Department.)

Four

THE ST. HELENA POLICE DEPARTMENT

The city of St. Helena was first settled by Dr. Edward Bale, who was granted the land from the Mexican government. Bale went on to build the Bale gristmill just outside St. Helena in 1846; the structure still stands today and is a state historic landmark.

St. Helena was incorporated in 1876; its first marshal was John H. Allison. The marshal and an elected constable policed the city in the early years.

In 1886, citizens complained about loud and profane prisoners in the city's jail; the town council contemplated gagging the prisoners until the city attorney deemed the idea illegal. The city instead built a sturdy stone jail with several cells. Minor criminals were housed in the jail to avoid the difficulty of transporting them to the county jail in the city of Napa. The jail stood until it was demolished in 1960 to make way for a parochial school.

The last known lynching in Napa County occurred in St. Helena on May 9, 1888. John Wright was being held in the town's jail, pending trial for a murder. Marshal Swartout heard rumors of trouble, so he left the keys to the jail with the local justice of the peace, Judge Elgin. In the middle of the night, a mob forced Elgin to produce the keys; the mob removed Wright from the jail and hanged him from a bridge near the Beringer Vineyard. The identities of the members of the mob were never discovered.

The St. Helena Police Department was first organized in 1940; the first chief of police was Chanie C. Johnson. He supervised a department of three officers. Until 1965, officers were summoned by means of a pole with a red light on top, which was located in the 1300 block of Main Street.

The St. Helena Police Department currently employs 10 sworn officers and 6 support personnel. The current chief of police is Monty Castillo.

The St. Helena town jail was constructed in 1886. It was built of sturdy stone construction to assuage complaints from citizens that the guests of the prior jail were too loud. Petty criminals and drunks were housed in its cells in lieu of being transported to the main county jail in the city of Napa. The jail was demolished in 1960 to make way for a new parochial school. (Author's collection.)

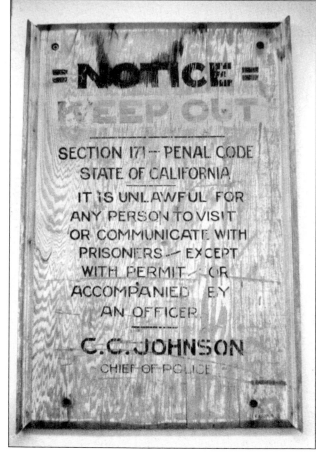

This sign was posted on the outside of St. Helena's jailhouse by Chief Chanie Johnson. The irony of the "keep out" sign was not lost on the *Ripley's Believe It or Not!* publishers, who included it in their book. The sign now hangs in the briefing room of the St. Helena Police Department. (Author's collection.)

Ken Hively served as an officer during the four years leading up to World War II. He went on to become the chief of police in the city of Calistoga upon his return from the war. In this 1940 photograph, Hively poses with his daughter, Patricia. (Courtesy of Beverly Hively.)

This 1937 Ford V-8 was the one and only patrol car for the St. Helena Police Department in 1940; it is pictured in front of the city hall. This photograph illustrates the minimal amount of police equipment on patrol vehicles of the time. Two-way radios were not yet being used. (Courtesy of the St. Helena Police Department.)

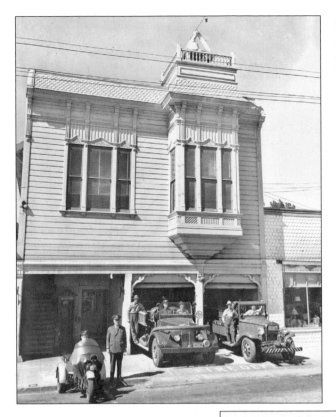

Members of the St. Helena Police and Fire Departments pose in front of city hall in 1947. This building was located on the west side of Main Street and housed not only city hall but the police and fire departments as well. Police chief Chanie Johnson is second from the left; Johnson served as chief from 1940 to 1952. (Courtesy of the St. Helena Fire Department.)

This rather plain-looking shoulder patch was standard issue during the 1950s and 1960s. It featured a blue background with yellow highlights. As in St. Helena, most departments in Napa County went without shoulder patches until the 1950s. (Courtesy of the St. Helena Police Department.)

Chief Etzio Ghiringhelli demonstrates a parking ticket payment system on Main Street in this late-1950s photograph. The "fine-o-meter" allowed citizens to pay for parking tickets directly at the meter. Chief Ghiringhelli led the department from 1956 to 1971. During the early years of his tenure, the department consisted of five officers and one patrol car. (Courtesy of the Robert E. McKenzie collection of the Napa Police Historical Society.)

Officer Harry Milani assesses the damage to the Montgomery Ward store at 1305 Main Street after an "unexpected customer" drove into the building in 1969. The elderly driver had been attempting to back out of a parking space across the street when he accidentally accelerated instead of braking. Luckily no one was injured during the incident. (Courtesy of Francis McMullen.)

This 1971 department photograph is deceptive; the officers wearing the helmets are actually reserve officers. There were only seven full-time officers at the time. Chief Arnold Harrison is seated third from the left. To the right of Chief Harrison is Sgt. Andy Angel; Angel succeeded Harrison as chief in 1974. In 1971, the department was first certified by the California Commission on Peace Officer Standards and Training (POST). (Courtesy of the St. Helena Police Department.)

Officer Dave Darling (left) received a certificate of training from St. Helena mayor Lowell Smith in 1976. Darling served St. Helena from 1970 to 2002. Darling's uniform sports a second-generation shoulder patch, which consisted of a black background with a gold seven-point star and burgundy city seal in the center; this patch was worn from 1971 to 1982. This patch was changed in 1983 to its current version. (Courtesy of Dave Darling.)

In the early 1980s, the shoulder patch of the department was changed. Chief James West asked his teenage son, an artist, to redesign the department vehicle's door decals to look similar to the patch. It was only after the decals were installed that word of mouth from St. Helena High School reached the department that the teen had included several unauthorized elements in the decal: the white hills in the background show a nude woman lying down, the word "pigs" is spelled out in the dark rows of grape crops, and an officer is visible in the clouds with an outstretched arm pointing a gun to the left. When the modifications were discovered, the decals were hastily replaced. (Courtesy of Mark Collins.)

This 1980 department photograph shows the force during the tenure of Chief of Police Andrew "AV" Angel (second row, with hat under arm). Chief Angel led the department from 1974 to 1983. He worked with Officer Steve Caouette to compile the first written history of the department in 1975. (Courtesy of the St. Helena Police Department.)

Officer Matt Talbott is show in this 1994 photograph with one of the department's alternative service vehicles, a 4-by-4 Chevrolet Blazer. Talbott is now a senior sergeant with the department and served as interim chief of police in 2006. (Courtesy of the St. Helena Police Department.)

St. Helena's current patrol cars feature a dynamic graphics pattern. The department has its own 24-hour dispatching; officers may also communicate with other agencies within Napa County via integrated radios. (Courtesy of the St. Helena Police Department.)

The current version of the St. Helena Police Department's shoulder patch features the cash crop of the Napa Valley prominently: grapes and vineyards. It was adopted by the department in 1983. (Courtesy of the St. Helena Police Department.)

The St. Helena Police Department appears in 2003. Chief Bert Johansson (eighth from the left) led the department from 1993 to 2003; he is the current St. Helena city manager. (Courtesy of the St. Helena Police Department.)

Five

THE CALISTOGA POLICE DEPARTMENT

The city of Calistoga began as an area called "Hot Springs," named after the naturally occurring springs in the area. In 1859, pioneer Samuel Brannan bought a one-square-mile area encompassing the springs. His goal was to develop the area into a tourist destination. Calistoga got its name during a banquet Brannan was hosting in the area in 1862. He tried to say he wanted to make the area the "Saratoga of California," alluding to a resort area he had known in New York. Instead Brannan said, "Calistoga of Sarifornia." The name stuck. In 1886, the city was incorporated.

The genesis of law enforcement in Calistoga mirrors that of other cities within the county. It was protected by an elected town marshal, who served a two-year term, and a night watchman. Cornelius H. Nash was elected as the first marshal. The city was also protected by a constable, an officer elected to serve the Calistoga Justice Court.

For many years, the police department worked out of the historic city hall located at 1232 Washington Street. The department occupied a small office on the back side of the building. A two-cell jail was located behind city hall; it served as the city's lockup for petty criminals until 1981. The jail still stands and serves as overflow storage for the city.

In 1912, an act of the state legislature changed the position of marshal from an elected one to one appointed by the city council. The position of marshal became known as the chief of police in 1922; Carl T. Pierce became the first chief. His force consisted of himself, a "night officer," and on occasion a "special" or "relief" officer (part-time positions). Officers were summoned by means of a light hanging at the center of the intersection of Lincoln and Washington Streets. Later a telephone booth was installed with a red-and-blue light on it; red if the call was for the fire department and blue if for the police.

Today the Calistoga Police Department is staffed by 10 sworn officers and 5 support personnel. The current chief of police is Jonathan Mills.

This is believed to be the first badge worn after the police department formed in the 1920s. Throughout much of its history, the department wore a standard seven-point badge with the California state seal in the center. Later the badge was changed to include a painted seal in the center. (Author's collection.)

Chief Carl T. Pierce led the department from 1922 to 1935; he is recognized as the first full-time chief of police. Prior to his appointment, the duties of chief were handled by the town marshal, who was elected every two years. (Courtesy of the Calistoga Police Department.)

Calistoga's city hall has been located in the same building since 1903. This 1948 photograph shows the one-stop nature of the building; it housed not only city hall but also the police department, fire department, and the tax collector. The police department took up 90 square feet at the rear of the building. Just behind city hall is a two-cell jailhouse, which was used until 1981. (Courtesy of the Calistoga Police Department.)

Police chief Ken Hively (left) was recruited by his predecessor, Chief Ed Light, to take over the department once Hively returned from service in World War II. Prior to the war, Hively served four years with the St. Helena Police Department. Pictured *c.* 1947 with Chief Hively is Officer Jay Hathaway, who later had a long career working as an investigator for the Federal Selective Services Board. (Courtesy of the Calistoga Police Department.)

In 1953, the Birleffi brothers, of Birleffi Motors, delivered a new Ford to Chief Hively (fourth from the left). This photograph illustrated the plainness of the department's uniforms at the time: tan shirt, khaki pants, and a seven-point gold badge. Later the same year, the department began wearing shoulder patches with an illustration of the Old Faithful geyser, a local tourist attraction; the same design is worn today. (Courtesy of the Calistoga Police Department.)

This photograph from the 1950s shows members of the department in the holiday spirit. Every holiday, members of the department work with community members to prepare and distribute food baskets to needy citizens. Chief Ken Hively is visible in the first row at far left.

Officer Jim Autry served more than 28 years with the department. Visible in this 1950s photograph is his signature pearl-handled revolver, which he wore in a cross-drawn holster. Autry went on to become the chief of police, serving as chief from 1971 to 1980. (Courtesy of the Calistoga Police Department.)

Retired boxer Henry Armstrong (left) meets with Chief Hively in 1955. Armstrong held four division titles at the same time and was inducted into the International Boxing Hall of Fame. Armstrong retired from boxing in 1945 and became an ordained Baptist minister. (Courtesy of Beverly Hively.)

Chief Ken Hively met several celebrities during his time as chief. In 1955, Chief Hively (right) served as a bodyguard for professional boxer Rocky Marciano (left) during his training in Calistoga. Chief Hively was in Marciano's corner during the second-to-last fight of Marciano's career, in San Francisco on May 16, 1955; it was Marciano's 40th knockout. (Courtesy of Beverly Hively.)

The aftermath of a 1961 traffic collision in downtown Calistoga is evident in this photograph. The motorist was observant of the caution sign concerning pedestrians; however, he missed the oncoming vehicle. (Courtesy of the Calistoga Police Department.)

Allen K. Bartlett (left) served a full career as a police officer in Southern California as a motorcycle officer before "retiring" to Calistoga. He joined the department in 1959 and served honorably until his second retirement in 1968. Here he is seen receiving a plaque in honor of his service to Calistoga. (Courtesy of the Calistoga Police Department.)

This 1970 photograph of Officer Mike Dick shows the standard uniform of the department at the time: a tan shirt and khaki pants. The uniform was changed to navy blue in the 1980s. (Courtesy of the Calistoga Police Department.)

Through the years, officers have had ancillary duties in addition to fighting crime. In this 1973 photograph, reserve officer Thomas Merek shows one of them, maintaining the city's parking meters. The lone graveyard officer in the 1940s was tasked with sweeping the streets three times a week. (Courtesy of the Calistoga Police Department.)

Gov. Ronald Reagan (left) meets with Chief Ken Hively (right) during a visit in Calistoga. Reagan served as California's third governor, from 1967 to 1975. Chief Hively met many celebrities and dignitaries who came to the city to visit its famous hot springs and spas. (Courtesy of Beverly Hively.)

This early-1970s photograph taken in front of city hall shows the relatively plain nature of police vehicle markings at the time: a simple gold foil badge on the door. The primary emergency equipment included a red "gumball" light with an integrated public address speaker. (Courtesy of the Calistoga Police Department.)

A unique off-road Jeep patrol vehicle served the department in the 1970s. The vehicle was particularly useful on rural roads and during flooding situations. It sported an orange paint scheme, two red-colored door post spotlights, and a growler-type siren. (Courtesy of the Calistoga Police Department.)

This 1985 group photograph includes several important people in Calistoga police history. The first full-time female officer was Carole Mobert Lilly (third from left), hired in 1980. To the left of Lilly is Sgt. Mike Dick, who would go on to become chief in 2002. Chief James Anderson is also pictured (second from right). (Courtesy of the Calistoga Police Department.)

Six

THE CALIFORNIA HIGHWAY PATROL

The California Highway Patrol in Napa County dates to 1917. At that time, Napa County sheriff Edward Kelton appointed Henry "Punch" Cavagnaro as Napa County's first "speed cop." Cavagnaro and Ramon Asedo made up the entire squad until 1919, when Cavagnaro was injured in a traffic accident. Until 1929, highway patrol units were county-based, with officers being hired by the local sheriff. The early Napa unit was known as the Napa County State Motor Patrol."

In 1929, the state centralized control of the CHP, placing it within the larger Department of Motor Vehicles. The CHP moved from a desk within the sheriff's department to its own office in downtown Napa, on Brown Street between Second and Third Streets. The office later moved to Division Street, then to its current location on the south side of the city of Napa on Golden Gate Drive. The Napa office now falls administratively under the larger Golden Gate Division within the CHP.

Brothers Jim and Melvin Critchley joined the Napa CHP in the mid-1920s. The brothers would both go on to long careers serving the citizens of Napa. Jim served as the area's captain, and Melvin went on to work over 40 years locally. Melvin retired as the most senior officer statewide with badge No. 1.

The Napa CHP office enforces traffic laws and investigates traffic accidents on the highways and unincorporated roadways of the county. In addition, the CHP provides investigative assistance when called upon by the Napa County Major Crimes Task Force.

The Napa CHP office has grown as the needs of the county have grown. Today 46 sworn officers and 6 support personnel are assigned to the office. The Napa CHP office is currently commanded by Capt. Mark Rasmussen.

Henry "Punch" Cavagnaro was first hired as a Napa County sheriff's deputy in 1906 to maintain order in a refugee camp set up after the San Francisco earthquake. In 1917, Sheriff Edward Kelton tapped Cavagnaro to become the county's first "speed cop"; he served in that capacity until a traffic collision sidelined him in 1919. Cavagnaro returned to the newly formed CHP in 1929, serving as a desk sergeant. (Courtesy of Art Cavagnaro.)

Officer Ramon Asedo is pictured astride his Harley-Davidson in this early-1920s photograph. Asedo was the second speed cop hired by Napa County sheriff Kelton. When Henry Cavagnaro was injured, Asedo assumed the role of captain; he supervised only one other officer at the time, Jim Critchley. Asedo perished in a small plane accident in 1926, near a baseball field east of the city of Napa. (Courtesy of Karen Asedo.)

Jim Critchley was hired in 1925 as Napa County's third speed cop. He was on the job only three months when his immediate supervisor, Capt. Ramon Asedo, was killed in an airplane accident. Critchley was promoted to captain and held that position until his retirement in 1954; he spent his entire career serving Napa County. (Courtesy of the Napa County Sheriff's Department.)

Members of the Napa County State Motor Patrol pose in this 1928 photograph. At this time, the CHP offices were still run at the county level; officers were hired by local sheriffs yet were paid by state funds. The Napa County "speed cops" worked out of the sheriff's department in the county courthouse. Pictured from left to right are Bart Freitas, Raymond "Midge" Raina, Melvin Critchley, and Jim Critchley. (Courtesy of Jim Critchley.)

10th Annual Convention, Californi
San Diego, Oct. 15 –

The 10th annual conference of the California Association of Highway Patrolmen (CAHP) was held in San Diego in October 1929. The CAHP was a fraternal organization that provided standardized training at its yearly conferences; it continues to be active today as the union bargaining unit for CHP officers and administers a widows and orphans fund to support relatives of slain officers.

The CHP had formally been organized as a statewide organization only two months prior to this conference. The variety of uniforms worn by county groups at the time is evident; the uniform was standardized in 1930. Napa County speed cops Melvin and Jim Critchley are visible in the second row, 10th and 11th from the left. (Courtesy of the California Highway Patrol, Napa Office.)

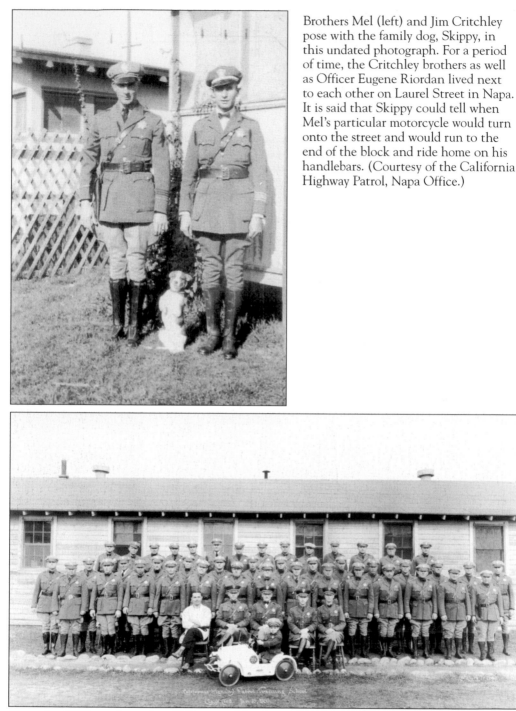

Brothers Mel (left) and Jim Critchley pose with the family dog, Skippy, in this undated photograph. For a period of time, the Critchley brothers as well as Officer Eugene Riordan lived next to each other on Laurel Street in Napa. It is said that Skippy could tell when Mel's particular motorcycle would turn onto the street and would run to the end of the block and ride home on his handlebars. (Courtesy of the California Highway Patrol, Napa Office.)

Once the CHP was formed in 1929, one of the first orders of business was to establish a training academy. Until this time, traffic officers had been trained on the job in their respective counties; training was sporadic and not standardized. Melvin Critchley, already on the job for four years, attended the eighth CHP academy in January 1930. Critchley is second from the left in the first row. (Courtesy of the California Highway Patrol, Napa Office.)

STATE OF CALIFORNIA
CALIFORNIA HIGHWAY PATROL
OF THE DEP/ ENT OF MOTOR VEHICLES
E. RA.MOND CATO, Chief

No. 1˙742

Driver _Loyd Wallace Nenta_ (PRINT NAME)   Oper. or Chauf. No. _69336_

Address _531 Wilson St Fresno_ (PRINT ADDRESS)   Make _Stude_

Owner _Same_   License No. _9B7032_

Address ____   Location _Oak St._

YOU ARE HEREBY NOTIFIED to appear before Justice of the Peace.

G Maynard   at _Napa_

10 a.m.
at 2 p.m. on the _24_ day of _June_ 193_2_, to answer charge/s of ____

violation/s of the California Vehicle Act of 1931; to wit: Sect./s ____ _113c_

(offense) _Speeding 60 - in 45_

I hereby promise to appear at the time and place mentioned.

Signed _L W Newton_   Address ____

Time of Arrest _7 30_ a.m./p.m.—Dated this _18_ day of _June_ 193_2_.

Signed _Bart J Freitas_   No. _88_
ARRESTING OFFICER

This 1932 traffic ticket demonstrates that speeders have been a problem ever since automobiles hit the streets. Officer Bart Freitas caught this driver going 60 miles per hour in a 45-mile-per-hour zone. Officers of the time estimated violator's speeds by pacing it in traffic; radar for police use did not appear until the 1950s. (Courtesy of the Napa County Sheriff's Department.)

In this 1933 photograph, Raymond "Midge" Raina poses with his Ford Model A patrol car in front of the Napa CHP office, located on Brown Street between Second and Third Streets. An illuminated globe light inscribed with the word "police" hangs above the door to the Napa Police Station, visible two businesses to the right. Napa City Hall is at the far right of the photograph. (Courtesy of the California Highway Patrol, Napa Office.)

Brothers Jim (left) and Mel Critchley work together to investigate a 1939 traffic accident. Mel's wooden baton is visible in the "sap pocket" of his trousers. Officers of the time typically carried a short baton, usually no longer than 10 or 12 inches. The CHP vehicle displays a door seal, which was used until 1947, when the CHP became autonomous from the Department of Motor Vehicles. (Courtesy of Don Critchley.)

Officer Bart Freitas investigates the aftermath of a fatal collision between a truck and a train in this 1940s photograph. The CHP is responsible for investigating any traffic collisions that occur in the unincorporated areas of the county. (Courtesy of the California Highway Patrol, Napa Office.)

City of Napa mayor Charles Trower (left) poses with Officer Joseph Mathews in this mid-1930s photograph. Officer Mathews has the distinction of being one of only two Napa CHP officers to die in the line of duty. In August 1939, Officers Joseph Mathews and Bart Freitas arrested several men who were fighting in the Vichy area of the county. Once they brought the men to the Napa CHP office, Mathews collapsed; he died the next day. It is believed his condition was aggravated by several on-duty traffic collisions Mathews had previously been involved in. Mathews, a Napa native, joined the CHP in 1930 and served his entire career in Napa County. (Courtesy of the California Highway Patrol, Napa Office.)

A 1947 awards presentation for motorcycle safety was presided over by CHP captain Jim Critchley (center). Present were Frank Barker (left) and motorcycle shop owner Nelson Bettencourt Jr. (right). The group is in front of the CHP office, which at the time was located within the Coca-Cola building on Division Street in the city of Napa. (Courtesy of Stan DeGarmo.)

This 1949 photograph of Officers Dixon and George Burton show two changes to the appearance of officers and their vehicle that resulted from the CHP separating from the Department of Motor Vehicles in 1947. First, the officers are wearing the newly adopted shoulder patch; previously officers wore a circular patch with spokes and a bear in the center. Second, the vehicle door decal was changed to a seven-point star. (Courtesy of the Napa Police Historical Society.)

Officer Al Southgate mugs for the camera in this mid-1950s photograph. Southgate spent all but 2 of his 26-year CHP career with the Napa office. He was an early member and president of the Napa County Peace Officer's Association. Southgate retired from the patrol in 1963. (Courtesy of the Robert E. McKenzie collection of the Napa Police Historical Society.)

Officers George Burton (left) and Al Southgate work together on a report inside the CHP office. At the time, the CHP and Department of Motor Vehicles were housed in the same office on Division Street, near downtown Napa. Burton joined the CHP in 1941 at the age of 39; the force had relaxed its age limits because of the shortage of able-bodied men during World War II. (Courtesy of Eleanor Lightner.)

The Napa CHP office is pictured as it appeared in 1955. Officers are, from left to right, W. E. Beck, Bart Freitas, Arnold French, George Burton, Vivian Biava, Al Southgate, Ed Rogers, Mel Critchley, Jim Dunaway, and Clarence Pieratt. Biava served as the office secretary for over 41 years. Pieratt was pinned against a road abutment on Redwood Road by a hit-and-run driver; one of his legs had to be amputated. (Courtesy of the California Highway Patrol, Napa Office.)

Members of the Napa CHP office line up for a yearly inspection by superiors from CHP headquarters in this 1958 photograph. Visible in the background are their Dodge Coronet patrol vehicles. The majority of the CHP's vehicles were two-door models until the early 1960s. (Courtesy of the Robert E. McKenzie collection of the Napa Police Historical Society.)

Melvin Critchley was forced to retire in 1969 when state law was changed to make 60 the maximum age for CHP officers. At the time, he had been on the force for over 40 years. When he retired, Critchley wore badge No. 1, meaning he was the most senior officer on the force. Badge No. 1 was retired with Critchley and now hangs at the CHP academy in West Sacramento. (Courtesy of the California Highway Patrol, Napa Office.)

This display at the CHP Academy Museum honors Officer Mel Critchley, the last person to wear badge No. 1. It also features group photographs of the Napa CHP office from 1928 and 1932. Currently new officers are assigned a badge number, which they carry with them during their entire career. (Author's collection.)

NAPA UNIT 1928
Bart Freitas, R. Raina, Mel Critchley, Jim Critchley "Captain"

NAPA UNIT 1932
R. Raina, Riordan, Bart Freitas, Biava, J. B. Critchley, Mathews, M. P. Critchley

Melvin P. Critchley

Badge #1 was worn for 43 years by California Traffic Officer Melvin P. Critchley.
He began his career with the Napa County Patrol on May 15, 1926 under California's Dual Control Agreement and continued service with the California Highway Patrol from the day of its formation August 14, 1929 until his retirement on January 2, 1969.

Officer George Butler was the second of two Napa CHP officers to die in the line of duty. On December 8, 1986, Butler was acting as an observer on a Napa-based CHP helicopter that was taking aerial photographs of a traffic collision in Solano County. When Butler got out of the helicopter to give the film to the patrol units, he was struck by the helicopter blade and killed instantly. Butler was a 20-year veteran of the CHP and had served eight years with the helicopter unit. The Butler Bridge in the southern part of Napa County was renamed in Officer Butler's honor. (Courtesy of the California Highway Patrol Academy.)

Seven

SPECIALIZED ENFORCEMENT

During the history of law enforcement in Napa County, there have arisen unique challenges because of institutions that have planted their roots in the valley. Several specialized agencies have been born over the years to meet these challenges.

The Napa State Mental Hospital accepted its first patients in 1875. Security of the hospital was initially handled by medical orderlies. In 1949, William Edwards became the hospital's first full-time security guard; he was known as a "watch keeper." The security force was expanded to five officers in 1962, with the addition of several officers who had prior police experience. In 1970, Stan Witten took over as chief of hospital security. He actively lobbied the state to give the security officers at Napa and other state mental hospitals peace officer status; in 1973, Witten's dream became a reality. Today the Napa State Hospital Police employs 113 sworn officers, making it the largest law enforcement agency within Napa County.

Napa Valley has been linked to the outside world by railroads since 1865. In 1987, private investors bought a portion of the rails between the cities of Napa and St. Helena. The section has been reborn as a venue for the popular "wine train" excursions. The Napa Railroad Police Department was first formed as a public safety department in 1989; it became a police department in 1999. The department protects passengers, employees, and freight along the entire right-of-way of the railroad; it currently employs three sworn officers.

Napa Valley Community College is located just south of the city of Napa; it hosts a daily population of 5,000 staff and students. The Napa Valley College Police Department was formed in 1997 to protect the students, staff, and property. It employs five sworn officers and four support personnel. In 1983, the college was certified by the state to host a police academy. Through the years, the academy has trained more than 2,900 cadets.

The dedicated men and women of these agencies have served in their unique roles over the years, allowing other agencies within the county to focus on more general policing.

The patrol units of the Napa Valley Railroad Police Department are shown in front of the "wine train." In 1987, the right-of-way for the wine train was purchased by Vincent DeDomenico, owner of the Golden Grain Macaroni Company and Ghirardelli Chocolate Company. The train uses refurbished vintage Pullman cars from 1915 to 1950, as well as a 1950 dome vista car. (Courtesy of the Napa Valley College Police Academy.)

The Napa Valley Railroad Police badge stands apart from the badges of other agencies within Napa County for two reasons: first, it is the only shield-type badge currently being used within the county. Second, it is the only badge to make use of two types of metals, a silver background and gold center. (Courtesy of the Napa Valley College Police Academy.)

A patrol unit of the Napa Valley College Police Department is parked in front of the temporary police station. The department is slated to move into a new facility in 2012. The college police patrol a sprawling campus that hosts an average population of 5,000 people every day. (Courtesy of Napa Valley College Police Department.)

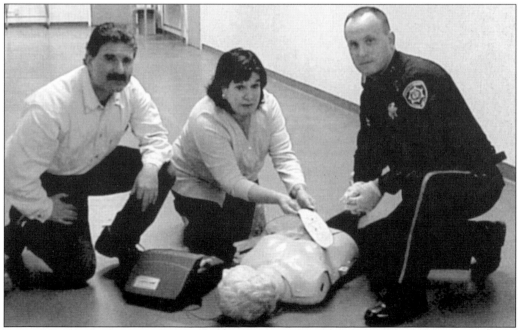

Napa Valley College police officer Mike Grimes (far right) trains with a newly acquired automatic external defibrillator (AED). The college police was the first department in Napa County to put AEDs in their patrol units. (Courtesy of Napa Valley College Police Department.)

Napa Valley College police officer Therese Johnson (left) talks to a student while riding a department-issued Segway personal transporter. The Segway's ability to traverse the narrow walkways of the college makes it an ideal way to patrol the sprawling campus. (Courtesy of Napa Valley College Police Department.)

Cadets at the police academy stand tall for inspection in 1995. Of note is Cadet David Orth in the foreground, wearing the white shirt. The base commander at Travis Air Force base sent security police personnel to the academy to be cross-trained during a short-lived program. Also visible in this photograph is Cadet Gregg Lee (far left); Lee now works for the Napa Police Department as a motorcycle officer. (Courtesy of the Napa Valley College Police Academy.)

Police academy cadets of class number 53 learn the importance of proper weapons cleaning after a day of shooting at the range. Cadets can be seen cleaning a workhorse of law enforcement, the pump-action shotgun. The shotgun has been phased out in many departments in recent years in favor of military-style patrol carbines, such as the AR-15. (Courtesy of the Napa Valley College Police Academy.)

Cadets attending the Napa Valley College Police Academy are required to undergo exposure to chemical agents, such as pepper spray. In the exercise pictured, the cadet has been sprayed and is working through the discomfort to handcuff a suspect. Cross-contamination of officers is common when chemical agents are used on patrol. (Courtesy of the Napa Valley College Police Academy.)

Napa State Hospital security officer Bob Wells (left) investigates a break-in on hospital property with Napa County sheriff's detective Joe Page (right). Wells worked as a night deputy with the sheriff's department for three years before being hired by the state hospital in 1962. Through the years, the sheriff's department has assisted state hospital personnel by investigating deaths and other serious crimes on the grounds of the hospital. (Courtesy of the Napa County Sheriff's Department.)

William Cunningham was one of four security officers hired in 1962 to assist William Edwards, who had served as the lone officer for 13 years. Cunningham formerly served as a military policeman during World War II, a highway patrolman in Connecticut, a criminal investigator at the Benicia Arsenal, and the chief of police for the Suisun City Police Department. (Courtesy of Royce Cunningham.)

This group photograph from 1994 captured several trendsetters within the department. Chief Jim Stratton (second from left, wearing hat) served during the transition from a hospital security to hospital police department. Brian Sallade (rear, with beard) became the first sergeant in 1988. Denise Daly (center) became the first female sergeant in 1996. (Courtesy of the Napa State Hospital Police Department.)

Officers perform law enforcement and correctional officer duties. Besides patrolling the state hospital ground via bicycle and vehicles, officers also provide site security for a portion of the hospital that houses patients who have committed various crimes and been found criminally insane, monitor the visitor center, transport patients to and from off-site court and medical facilities, and maintains an investigations bureau. This photograph shows part of the department's correctional duties: Officer Sam Dedios monitors the vehicle "sally port" entry into the secure area of the hospital. (Courtesy of the Napa State Hospital Police Department.)

This photograph highlights the varied job duties of officers. A current patrol sits ready for action; it is used in the department's law enforcement function to patrol the vast ground of the state hospital. The patrol car is parked in front of one of the department's transportation vans, used to transport patients to off-site medical and court appointments. (Courtesy of the Napa State Hospital Police Department.)

Eight

WORKING TOGETHER

Throughout the history of organized law enforcement in Napa County, the officers of the various departments have consistently maintained close working relationships. Early in the county's history, working together was a necessity. The sheriff and one deputy were responsible for policing the entire unincorporated area of the valley; they frequently called on the town marshal or constable to assist them. Napa County is also geographically isolated; this fact was even more apparent before the advent of the automobile. A call for aid to an officer in neighboring Sonoma or Solano County today can be answered within minutes; the trip might have taken an entire day by horseback.

Napa County's narcotics task force, the Napa Special Investigations Bureau (NSIB), was first formed in 1977. It is supervised by an agent from the California Bureau of Narcotics Enforcement and consists of members on loan from the Napa Police and Sheriff's Departments. Each year, NSIB locates and eradicates marijuana gardens and diligently works to stem the flow of narcotics into the county.

Napa County employs a multiagency taskforce when a major crime, such as a homicide, occurs. The Napa County Major Crimes Taskforce brings together investigators from each police department, the sheriff's department, and the CHP, as well as district attorneys' investigators. The taskforce concept has proven very valuable by allowing a large number of investigators, each of whom brings their own expertise, to work collaboratively.

In addition to these formal working partnerships, the history of policing the county is littered with acts of selflessness and cooperation. Officers from various departments have come together to help charity causes, to support families of officers who have been hurt or killed in the line of duty, to train each other on the latest enforcement techniques, and in their daily duties patrolling the county. While officers may wear many different uniforms, they realize they all serve for similar purposes and daily stand in the gap to protect the citizens of Napa County.

Napa police chief Sherwood Munk (left) and Napa County sheriff John Claussen (right) share a moment during a joint event in which contraband slot machines were destroyed. Chief Munk and Sheriff Claussen led their respective departments during the booming post–World War II period. Both held their posts until 1967. (Courtesy of the Napa Police Historical Society.)

Members of the Napa County law enforcement community come together for a funeral service at Tulocay Cemetery in this late-1950s photograph. Among the attendees are Napa County sheriff John Claussen (far left), CHP officer Mel Critchley (next to Claussen), and future Napa police chief Ken Jennings (third from the left in dark uniform). (Courtesy of the Robert E. McKenzie collection of the Napa Police Historical Society.)

Napa County sheriff's deputy Bob Wells (left) and Napa police officer Stanley "Bill" Johnson (right) pose in front of an informational display for the Napa County Peace Officers Association during a 1950s Napa County Fair. Deputy Wells is wearing his department-issued felt hat, a style worn through the 1950s. (Courtesy of the Napa County Sheriff's Department.)

The Napa County Peace Officers Association (NCPOA) was formed in 1949 as a fraternal organization. Members in this 1958 photograph are, from left to right, CHP officer Al Southgate, Napa County sheriff's deputy John Dellagana, and Napa police officer Elmer Stahl. The NCPOA is still active today and offers a death benefit to the families of officers who die in the line of duty. (Courtesy of the Robert E. McKenzie collection of the Napa Police Historical Society.)

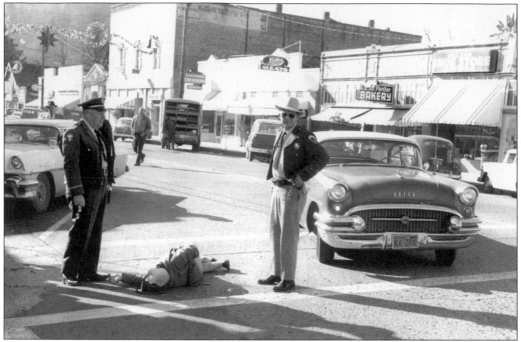

Calistoga police chief Ken Hively (left) works with Napa County sheriff's deputy Al Lindholm to investigate a fatal vehicle-versus-pedestrian accident in downtown Calistoga in 1962. Sheriff's deputies act as deputy coroners during death investigations. Napa County elected a civilian coroner until 1969, when Sheriff Earl Randol became the first sheriff-coroner. (Courtesy of the Napa County Sheriff's Department.)

Every Napa County agency, as well as members of the public and military, turned out in March 1963 to search for a missing five-year-old girl, Doreen Heskett. The search included grid searches of fields, tracking with dogs, and aerial searches. Doreen was not located until nine months later; her body was found in a field south of the city of Napa. The case remains an open "cold case" homicide. (Courtesy of the Robert E. McKenzie collection of the Napa Police Historical Society.)

The leaders of three agencies confer in this mid-1960s photograph. Pictured from left to right are Napa County sheriff's deputy Bob Cozad, Calistoga police chief Ken Hively, Sheriff John Claussen, St. Helena police chief Etzio Ghiringhelli, and sheriff's deputy Ray Land. (Courtesy of the Napa County Sheriff's Department.)

The Junior Traffic Patrol was created in 1955. Each elementary school is assigned an officer to organize students to act as crossing guards at their respective schools. At the end of the year, every school's unit meets for the traffic patrol review, held at Napa Memorial Stadium. Dignitaries at the 1964 review were, from left to right, CHP captain Burke, Undersheriff Gardner, Judge Blankenship, Napa Chief Munk, and Officer Holden. (Courtesy of the Napa Police Historical Society.)

Officers from several Napa County agencies join together during an event for the American Cancer Society in 1967. Pictured from left to right are CHP sergeant Ken Forster, Napa police officer Frank Madalena, American Cancer Society volunteer Tina Wolfe, and Napa sheriff's captain Joe Page. (Courtesy of the Napa County Sheriff's Department.)

Napa police chief Ken Jennings (left) and Napa County sheriff Earl Randol pose after a 1970 charity basketball game held between the NPD and Napa County Sheriff's Department; the NPD team won the game. (Courtesy of the Napa Police Historical Society.)

The Napa Special Investigations Bureau (NSIB) was formed in 1977; it is Napa County's narcotics taskforce. The charter members posed for this photograph after a successful drug bust in downtown Napa. They are, from left to right, NPD officer Vince Ghiringhelli, Deputy Steve Parson, NPD officer Mike Roth, state agent Mike Gilbert, Deputy John Baumgartner, D. A. Investigator Mike Chouinard, and NPD officer Larry Rupp. (Courtesy of Mike Chouinard.)

Members of the Napa Police and Sheriff's Departments joined forces to battle Napa County firefighters in the 1980 police and fire benefit football game. This was the third year the charity game was played; it ended in a 14-14 tie. The law enforcement team played in various games through 1983, versus both firefighter and law enforcement teams from other counties. (Courtesy of Janet Lipsey.)

Napa sheriff's deputy Bill McGlothern (left), Napa police officer Ron Allgower (center), and Napa sheriff's deputy Rick Robben (right) pose during a mid-1980s stint at CAMP. Created in 1983, CAMP stands for Campaign Against Marijuana Planting and is run by the California Bureau of Narcotics Enforcement. (Courtesy of the Napa Police Historical Society.)

Napa Special Investigations Bureau (NSIB) members Napa police officers Bill Jabin (left) and Joe Matulich (right) are shown with a bumper crop of marijuana confiscated from a clandestine growing operation. Every year, NSIB members locate and eradicate numerous marijuana crops, mostly in the unincorporated areas of the county. (Courtesy of the Napa Police Historical Society.)

Napa Valley Register photographer Robert E. McKenzie, Bob to his friends, took many of the photographs in this book during his 36 years with the newspaper, spanning the 1950s to the 1990s. He was well-known and well liked by the entire Napa County law enforcement community. Bob's photographs of crime and accident scenes many times became evidence in the years before the various departments employed their own photographers. (Courtesy of the Robert E. McKenzie collection of the Napa Police Historical Society.)

The Napa police and sheriff join forces to provide crowd control during a pro-choice demonstration in front of a pro-life meeting place in 1993. Napa County agencies frequently work together to bolster their numbers during large events. The Napa sheriffs, Napa police, and the California Highway Patrol provided security during a 2006 visit of Pres. George W. Bush. (Courtesy of the Napa Police Historical Society.)

The Napa Police and Sheriff Departments' SWAT teams frequently train together and are available for mutual assistance during major incidents. In this 2003 photograph, the teams participate in a mock terrorism training exercise that required them to act while dressed in protective equipment. The Napa Police SWAT vehicle (left) is a converted bank armored car; it first entered service in 1997. (Courtesy of the Napa Valley College Police Academy.)

The Napa Police dispatch center has provided dispatch services to several agencies since it was consolidated in 1979. It provides call taking and dispatching for the NPD, sheriff, the contract police cities of American Canyon and Yountville, and the Napa City and County Fire Departments. The center also answers all 911 calls in the county except those from cellular phones. The center uses computer-aided dispatching and global positioning tracking of patrol cars to provide better service. (Author's collection.)

Nine

NAPA'S MOST WANTED

Ever since the beginning of the recorded history of Napa County, there have been a select few who have chosen to disregard the law and commit crimes for their own nefarious reasons. For just as long, there have been men willing to pin on a badge and bring these outlaws to justice.

At the start of Napa County, bringing criminals to justice was a haphazard prospect. Napa lacked a courthouse and a jail. The first recorded suspects arrested for murder in 1850 had to be housed in the old adobe jail in Sonoma; their trial was presided over by Judge Stephen Cooper, who was based out of the then–state capital, Benicia.

Napa County throughout its history has enjoyed relatively low crime rates. It is not uncommon for there to be no murders anywhere in the county for months or years at a time; however, the potential for violence is ever present.

Through the years, Napa County has seen several milestones in the annals of California criminal justice history, including holding the last public execution in the state. Infamous criminals such as Buck English and "The Zodiac" have plied its roads.

Historically when violent crimes have occurred, the law enforcement of Napa County has concentrated its efforts to catch the perpetrator. From the early days of brave men forming posses to track down stagecoach robbers and murders to the current Napa County Major Crimes Taskforce, Napa County law enforcement has a long history of working together to protect the citizens of the county.

From a photograph by the London Stereoscopic and Photographic Company

In 1874, Eadweard Muybridge, a noted photographer who worked with Leland Stanford, learned that his much-younger wife was having an affair with Maj. Harry Larkyns. Muybridge found Larkyns at the Yellowjacket Mining Camp, west of Calistoga. When Larkyns answered the door, Muybridge said, "Hello Larkyns, here is a message from my wife," and shot and killed him. Muybridge was immediately arrested; however, after a trial, he was found not guilty. The jury ruled the killing to be "justifiable." Muybridge went on to create the zoopraxiscope, a device that played a series of still photographs in rapid succession, a precursor to modern motion pictures. (Courtesy of the University of Pennsylvania Archives.)

116

16426

Laurence English

Robbery

Life

Napa

Buck English was a notorious Lake County bandit. In 1895, he and R. N. Breckenridge robbed a stagecoach traveling between Lake and Napa Counties. The sheriff in Napa was alerted that English and Breckenridge were en route to Napa via Monticello Road; a posse was raised and started to meet them. The posse confronted the bandits and a gunfight ensued. English shot at Undersheriff Robert Brownlee, the bullet striking the stock of Brownlee's shotgun. English was shot and severely wounded during the confrontation. English was sentenced to life, Breckenridge to 25 years; they both served their terms at San Quentin State Prison. English was released in 1912, Breckenridge in 1910. (Courtesy of the California State Archives.)

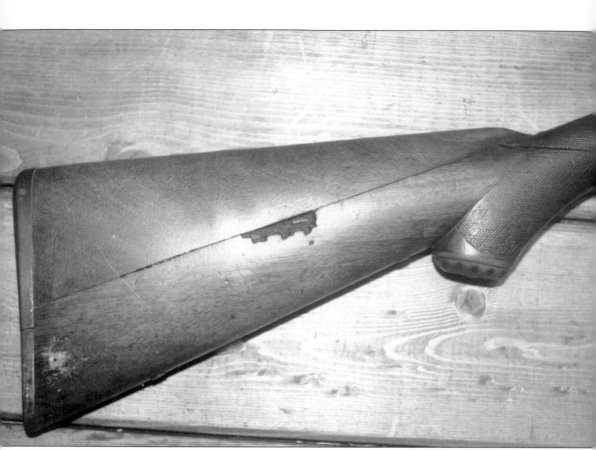

The shotgun that probably saved Undersheriff Brownlee's life during his shoot-out with Buck English is on display at the Napa County Sheriff's Department Museum. The area on the shotgun's stock where the bullet struck is clearly visible. In an odd footnote of history, Buck English's older brother Daniel met an untimely death during a shoot-out in a dance hall in the Spanishtown area of the city of Napa in 1868. Earlier on the night of his death, Daniel English and another of English's brothers had tried to rob John Lonergan, shooting at him five times; Lonergan only escaped by jumping into the Napa River. John Lonergan is the great-grandfather of now-retired Napa police officer Dan Lonergan and Napa County undersheriff Richard Lonergan. (Author's collection.)

On February 9, 1891, the peace of the Greenwood house was shattered when two would-be robbers, William Roe and Charles Schmidt, attempted to force the owner, Capt. John Greenwood, to give them money. Angered by the lack of money at the house, the robbers forced Greenwood and his wife, Lucina, to drink chloroform and then shot both of them. Lucina died, but Captain Greenwood miraculously survived his three gunshot wounds. The killers fled the area; Schmidt was caught a year later, Roe six years later. The house originally stood south of the city of Napa, on land at the southeast corner of what is now Highway 29 and Jamison Canyon Road. In 1990, it was moved a short distance west, to its current location at the intersection of Airport and Devlin Roads. Visible in the background of this contemporary photograph is the new Napa County Sheriff's Department, opened in 2005. (Author's collection.)

$4,500 REWARD.

Wanted for Murder and Robbery.

The above reward will be paid for the arrest and conviction of the two men who killed Mrs. Greenwood and robbed the house of J. Q. Greenwood, in Napa County, February 9th, 1891.

DESCRIPTION OF MEN.

The American is about 5 feet 9 inches high; between 30 and 40 years of age; high cheek bones; rather narrow chin; slim build; wrinkles on his neck; dark complexion; looks like a drinking man; dark brown hair; dark mustache; wore gold chain, with broad, flat fob attached; wore a full suit of brown, sack coat, slouch black felt hat, rather high crown, and light-colored overcoat. He is supposed to wear ring on third finger of right hand, with dark stone setting in same. He took a pair of kip boots, well worn, No. 7, split-leather backs and backs rough, as is often the case with split leather; wore red socks.

The Swede (supposed to be Swede or German) is about 5 feet 10 inches high; 25 or 30 years old; square build; round face; small eyes; light complexion; light hair and mustache; wore dark blue suit; white shirt; felt hat, with low crown and round top, brim broad and inclined to be flat; supposed to wear an old, dark gray, shoddy, cheviot ulster overcoat.

GEO. S. McKENZIE, Sheriff,

Napa, February 10th, 1891.

Napa, Cal.

14980
Carl Schmidt
Murder 1st degree
Life
Napa

In response to the killing of Lucina Greenwood, Napa County sheriff George McKenzie sent out scores of these "wanted" postcards to law enforcement agencies across California and beyond. It was a common practice of the time to send these types of postcards for anything from horse thievery to murder. (Courtesy of the Napa County Sheriff's Department.)

Carl Schmidt was one of two robbers who attacked Captain Greenwood and his wife in 1891. Schmidt fled California; however, he turned himself in to the Denver police in 1892. Schmidt claimed he met his partner, William Roe, a day before the botched robbery and murder. He was returned to Napa, tried and convicted of murder, and was sent to San Quentin State Prison; he died there in 1957. (Courtesy of the California State Archives.)

UNDER NO CONSIDERATION IS THIS PASS TRANSFERABLE.

Napa, Cal., January 1, 1897.

Mr. *R. S. Bell*

You are respectfully invited to be present at the official execution of

WILLIAM M. ROE

which will take place at the County Jail in Napa, on the 15th day of January, 1897, at 11 o'clock A. M. SHARP.

Geo. S. McKenzie

Sheriff of Napa Co., Cal.

o one admitted without this Card.

In 1896, William Roe had been on the run for five years after murdering Lucina Greenwood. One night, he was drinking at a bar in San Fernando, California, when he confided in the bartender that he was a murderer. Unfortunately for Roe, the bartender was W. B. Schaug, a former deputy U.S. marshal. Roe was arrested, returned to Napa, and convicted of murder. He was sentenced to be hanged outside the courthouse in the city of Napa. Napa sheriff George McKenzie sent out 400 invitations to area lawmen and noted citizens; women were not allowed. This was the last public execution in California. The gallows used during the execution are now on display at the Napa County Sheriff's Department's museum. (Courtesy of the Napa County Sheriff's Department.)

The assembled witnesses prepare to view the execution of William Roe. Visible in the background is the fence and canvas tarp used to shield the spectacle from unwanted eyes. California passed a law in 1891 mandating that all executions occur at San Quentin State Prison; however, because the killing of Lucina Greenwood occurred before the law was passed, the 1897 execution was allowed to occur in Napa. (Courtesy of the Napa County Sheriff's Department.)

This chilling photograph from January 15, 1897, captures the moment the trap door opened during the execution of William Roe. A 20-foot-tall fence was erected around the witness viewing area, and a canvas tarp was stretched over the top in order to prevent others from viewing the spectacle. Napa County sheriff George McKenzie is visible holding his right arm up, to the right of Roe's moving body. (Courtesy of the Napa County Sheriff's Department.)

This photograph captures the moments after the death sentence
had been carried out. Sheriff McKenzie holds a knife, preparing
to cut William Roe down. Roe's coffin is prepared to receive him
directly below. Dr. Edwin Hennessey is pictured to the right of Sheriff
McKenzie. Dr. Hennessey helped organize the first hospital in Napa
County and was a pioneer in the use of X-rays. (Courtesy of the Napa
County Sheriff's Department.)

Paul Chaigneau has the unfortunate distinction of being the only
chief of police in Napa County to spend time behind bars. Chaigneau
was Napa town marshal/chief of police from 1892 to 1899. He was
convicted of embezzling funds he collected as part of his duties as
marshal. Chaigneau served one year at San Quentin State Prison. The
photograph below shows Chaigneau on the day he entered prison; the
top two show him on the day of his release. (Courtesy of the California
State Archives.)

Tools of safecrackers were recovered after a wild chase through Napa in 1948. While being transported to the police station, the two suspects, Thomas Fargo and John De La Casa, pulled out guns. De La Casa shot Officer Willis Hill in the leg before jumping from the car. Fargo faced the barrel of Officer John McGylnn's revolver and was shot five times; Fargo survived and was sent to San Quentin. (Courtesy of the Robert E. McKenzie collection of the Napa Police Historical Society.)

WANTED

FOR ASSAULT TO COMMIT MURDER

John J. De La Casa
John J. delacasa alias
John Ross
John Morgan
Jack Drake
Jack Dale
Jack De La Casa

F.B.I.   #280833
McNeil Island   UN 8235
Colorado St. Penn   17641
U.S.P. Lynwth. Kan.   30854

F.P.C.   25   12
         17 A 12

Ref.   9   U
       17 A

Description: White, Male, 43 6-1/2 180 Hair dark, Eyes dark.

WANTED for the shooting of two Police Officers here. October 17, 1948, at Napa, California.

We hold felony Warrant.

Bail $150,000.00   Cash $300,000.00   Surety.

Arrest, hold, wire collect. We will extradite.

Use extreme caution in apprehending.

EUGENE C. RIORDAN
Chief of Police
Napa, California

De La Casa led officers on a chase across the city, carjacking five vehicles and wounding Deputy George Gordon before disappearing. This "wanted" flyer for him was sent to law enforcement throughout the state after the shootings. Three months after the Napa shootings, De La Casa's luck ran out. In January 1949, he was killed during a shoot-out with the Los Angeles Police Department after he tried to rob a teenager; De La Casa wounded three officers in the gun battle. (Courtesy of the Napa Police Historical Society.)

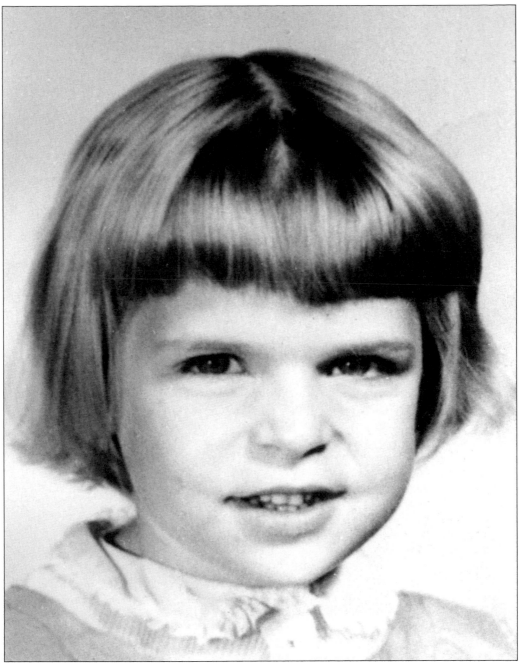

On March 25, 1963, the innocence of Napa was lost when five-year-old Doreen Heskett went missing while walking to a friend's house. A massive search ensued, covering the entire city of Napa. The use of military personnel, search helicopter and airplanes, civilians, and bloodhounds failed to turn up any sign of Heskett. Nine months later, Heskett's body was found in a farm field just south of the city of Napa. Scores of potential suspects were questioned; however, there was insufficient evidence to charge anyone with the murder. The case remains an unsolved "cold case" homicide. (Courtesy of the Napa Police Historical Society.)

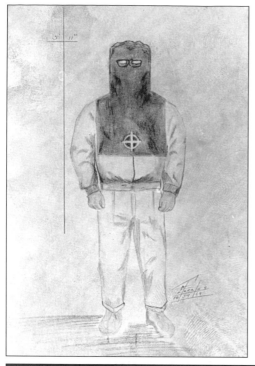

On September 27, 1969, Bryan Hartnell and Cecilia Shepard were picnicking at Lake Berryessa in eastern Napa County. A hooded man armed with a handgun and knife confronted them. Once they were tied up, the man stabbed them both, leaving them for dead. Hartnell survived and was found by a passing fisherman; Shepard died at the hospital. Hartnell worked with an artist to produce this image of his attacker. (Courtesy of the Napa County Sheriff's Department.)

After he attacked Bryan Hartnell and Cecilia Shepard, their assailant drew graffiti on Hartnell's vehicle. The symbol tied the crime to the "Zodiac" serial killer; the dates drawn corresponded to dates of Zodiac murders. Napa sheriff's deputy Joe Page (left) assisted Det. Hal Snook (right) as he processed Hartnell's vehicle for fingerprints. This door is still maintained as evidence at the sheriff's department. (Courtesy of the Napa County Sheriff's Department.)

NAPA COUNTY LAW ENFORCEMENT MORTALITY ROSTER

NAME	DEPARTMENT	END OF WATCH
Chief Alexander Herritt	Napa Police Department	January 25, 1933
Officer Joseph Mathews	California Highway Patrol	August 10, 1939
Officer Henry O. Rockstroh	Calistoga Police Department	July 20, 1940
Officer George Butler	California Highway Patrol	December 8, 1986
Sgt. Michael Roth	Napa Police Department	March 13, 1987

ACROSS AMERICA, PEOPLE ARE DISCOVERING SOMETHING WONDERFUL. *THEIR HERITAGE.*

Arcadia Publishing is the leading local history publisher in the United States. With more than 3,000 titles in print and hundreds of new titles released every year, Arcadia has extensive specialized experience chronicling the history of communities and celebrating America's hidden stories, bringing to life the people, places, and events from the past. To discover the history of other communities across the nation, please visit:

www.arcadiapublishing.com

Customized search tools allow you to find regional history books about the town where you grew up, the cities where your friends and family live, the town where your parents met, or even that retirement spot you've been dreaming about.